"So cute"

"2 gEnius"

"beautiful...and smart!"

"Look--2 teeth!"

BOOKS BY LOIS WYSE

Nonfiction

Company Manners

The Six-Figure Woman

Lovetalk

Mrs. Success

Funny, You Don't Look Like a Grandmother

Kid, You Sing My Songs

Grandchildren Are So Much Fun, I Should Have Had
Them First

Grandmother's Treasures

You Wouldn't Believe What My Grandchild Did . . .

Fiction

The Granddaughter

Far from Innocence

Kiss, Inc.

The Rosemary Touch

Seconds

Poetry

Love Poems for the Very Married

Are You Sure You Love Me?

A Weeping Eye Can Never See

Love Poems for a Rainy Day

S I M O N   &   S C H U S T E R
New York London Toronto Sydney Tokyo Singapore

You wouldn't believe what my Grandchild did...

by
Lois Wyse

Illustrated by Lilla Rogers

SIMON & SCHUSTER
Rockefeller Center
1230 Avenue of the Americas
New York, New York 10020

SIMON & SCHUSTER and colophon are registered
trademarks of Simon & Schuster Inc.

Designed by Bonni Leon-Berman

Manufactured in the United States of America
1 3 5 7 9 10 8 6 4 2

Library of Congress Cataloging-in-Publication Data
Wyse, Lois.
You wouldn't believe what my grandchild did. . . / Lois Wyse.
p. cm.
1. Grandparent and child—Humor. 2. Grandparenting—
Humor. 3. Grandchildren—Humor. I. Title
PS3573. Y74Y63   1994
818' .5402—dc20   93-50911
ISBN: 0-671-89293-2   CIP

For the parents and grandparents

of the family of grandchildren

Lee and I will love forever

and for all those friends and teachers

who make the garden grow

With Thanks

I want to express loving thanks to my grandchildren and my children—the naturals, in-laws, step-, and step-in-laws—whose sweetness and support light my life; to my mother, who is at the root of our stories; and to the most extraordinary group of friends any woman ever had.

Both professionally and personally I thank John Mack Carter, the editor-in-chief of *Good Housekeeping*, who made it possible for me to find my voice and say my piece about "The Way We Are" in the pages of that magazine; my appreciation also to Rick Bowers, the editor who first thought it would be a good idea for me to write a weekly syndicated newspaper column for Maturity News Service; particular thanks to Edward J. Acton, who, as my literary agent and caring friend, has always tried to find the right home for me; to Carolyn Reidy, who believes in the importance of writing about relationships; and to Laurie Bernstein, who is too young to be a grandmother but is old enough to be a particularly savvy and sentimental editor.

I am also grateful to those families whose stories are the basis for this book—friends of my daily life and friends I know only through their warm responses to the things I write.

New York

L.W.

1994

Contents

11

Part Two

Miami, Your-Ami, Her-Ami; or My Grandparents the Tourist Attraction

Part Three

Family Ties; or Unsnarling the Married, Unmarried, Almost Married World of Parents, Children, and Grandchildren

Part Four

Heartstrings

13

Introduction

*N*ow that women like Elizabeth Taylor, Jacqueline Onassis, and Debbie Reynolds are grandmothers, people understand that grandmothers no longer have to look like those little roly-poly grannies in first-grade readers.

We don't have to wear round glasses and square shoes.

We don't have to bake cakes from scratch.

We don't need to sit around on rocking chairs, knitting and waiting for the world to pass us by.

We are a whole new generation of grandmothers and grandfathers, who exercise and eat carefully in order to feel fabulous and fool the calendar.

We work and we travel; we dance and we party.

But in our heart of hearts, we never forget that we are grandparents.

Our buzzwords are "condo," "Disneyland," and "yes."

Our grandchildren know, while still in the crib, that we are something else; we are totally different from their parents.

We know too, because we look at these new lives with a love that is not filled with the everyday anxiety of parenting. We realize that we are here to provide the soft edge to the hard rules mothers and fathers must enforce in order to raise children with some sense of order and responsibility in a chaotic world.

We understand the parents' role. After all, we've played it. We've been the policemen and the parole officers in the home. We've been the teachers and the trainers and the coaches.

camcorder

The Grandparents' Kit ✚

VISA
3501412 1

CHOCOLATE BAR

YUM!

Now it's recess time for us; we are ready for the fun period of raising kids.

Fun without all that responsibility.

Joy without jeopardy.

We learn about the promise of this new time in life with the birth of our first grandchild, then supplement that lore as each new baby is added.

My granddaughter Molly figured out grandmas the first time that she looked up at me, cooed and giggled, and I giggled back. She's seven now, and I'm still giggling. Why shouldn't I? I don't have to comb her hair or tell her to bathe, dress, eat, and do her homework.

Once when she was six or so and especially annoyed with her mother, she turned to me and asked, "Do you think that my mother will be as good to my children as you are to us? Will my mother give my kids chocolate and treats the way you do?"

"Of course she will," I assured her.

"I don't think so," Molly answered. "My mother is *so* strict. She probably wouldn't give them candy anytime they wanted or ice cream for breakfast."

"In that case," I told her solemnly, "I promise to hang around just for your children, and when your mother says no, I'll say yes and give them everything they want."

"Thanks, Grandma," Molly said with relief, and went back to play with her dolls.

That Molly story is proof that she understands what grandparents are supposed to do. I also have Marisa stories and

Elizabeth and Sarah stories, Noah, Max, and Alex stories, as well as Emily and Stephanie stories.

I tell and retell these stories, and in this way I help spin our family history. This is one of those things that all of us grandparents do. Despite camcorders and tape machines, we remain the human recorders of the events of our lives. For who can tell the smallest event of life and recount it with more loving detail than a grandparent? Who can embellish, embroider, and embrace facts more artfully than a granny or grandpa?

Despite our lithe bodies and active minds, we are old-fashioned in recounting brave and beautiful anecdotes, clever sayings and accomplishments of those we love.

A grandparent can do ten minutes on "Little Mikey and the School Christmas Pageant." A loose tooth is good for another seven minutes. And learning to walk, talk, and wave bye-bye can take longer than a four-part miniseries.

For grandparents, part of the fun of loving is the joy of telling about the grandchildren.

Parents are only beginners in the game of loving children.

Love, real generational love, comes with years of practice.

It is the best, and so it is saved for last.

It takes a pro to recognize that there is no love sweeter, more giving or forgiving, than that of grandparent for grandchild.

As more than one astute observer of the family scene has noted, "Parents discipline; grandparents spoil."

Since all this spoilage is today being administered by the largest group of grandparents the world has ever seen, one might

assume that the world is increasingly filled with rotten little kids.

But wonder of wonders, each grandchild is sweet as a gum-drop, cute as a button, smart as a whip.

I'm certain of that because I have never heard a grandparent who wasn't amazed by the brilliance and beauty of the newest generation. We rise as one to proclaim the superiority of our children's children; the only issue of contention is whose grandchild is the best and the brightest.

Sometimes we are amazed that the children we thought so difficult to raise have produced such remarkable children—and we are even more amazed that we are old enough to be the grandparents.

But grandparents we are, and we relish our second chance to watch our garden grow.

We realize that grandparenting, like life itself, is a series of stages.

There is the first-time grandparent, who longs to speak volumes and instead finds himself reduced to baby talk with a non-speaking person.

As grandchildren grow and more grandchildren arrive, we grandparents suddenly find ourselves in the role we thought our parents would play forever: the heads of the family, the owners of the holidays, the tellers of family tales.

As our grandchildren get older, we find ourselves back at school and in the middle of problems we've never encountered. We thought buying an encyclopedia was a big deal when we were

parents. Nowadays Baby not only needs a library of reference material, Baby needs a new computer. Suddenly it is Baby's turn to take the stage.

Once you have a grandchild, you know the stage will never be dark for you.

So curtain up. Light the lights.

In these pages it's center stage for grandparents, grandchildren, and, from time to time, our mutual enemy—the parents, that necessary bridge from grandparent to grandchild.

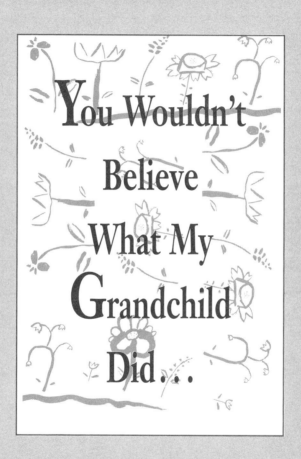

You Wouldn't Believe What My Grandchild Did...

Part ONE

Granny

GOES

Bonkers;

or

falling for
the new
kid
in
town.

So You're Going to Be a Grandmother!

ou picked up the tickets for the cruise, and you are eyeing the fabrics for redoing the bedroom, when you get the call. . . . "Mom, you're going to be a grandmother." After you cancel the tickets and send back the fabrics, you settle down and wait until you are told that it is now safe to notify the world.

You start spreading the news. . . .

Your husband is engrossed in watching the football game, so you wait through six downs and four offsides. "We're going to be grandparents," you announce portentously during a beer commercial. He doesn't even turn the sound down. "Did you hear me?" you repeat, and once again you say, "We're going—"

"Shhhhh," he responds. "I'm not ready."

Your mother gets very excited. She never dreamed she'd live to see a great-grandchild. Then the advice begins. She informs you that since she raised you so *perfectly*, she knows everything you'll need to know. Also, she was the *perfect* noninterfering grandmother and hopes you will be as *perfect* as she—although that is highly unlikely.

Your best friend, already a grandmother, tells you the best places to buy toys and very, very expensive baby clothes.

Your other best friend, not a grandmother, is jealous and admits it. She says that she thinks the reason her children are not having children is that it's the only way they can get even with her for having had them.

Your orthopedist advises you not to lift the baby once he weighs forty pounds. You assure him that will probably not be New Baby's birth weight.

Your real estate agent wastes no time in mentioning that the parents-to-be will probably have to move—and she has some terrific bargains. Of course, she's sure you'll want to help, so . . .

Your lawyer immediately suggests that you rewrite your will and reminds you to be sure to take care of the parent who is *your* child, because in case of divorce . . . You remind your lawyer that this couple is not dividing; they are multiplying. He shrugs and says it's too bad you're not as smart and experienced and distrustful as he.

Your banker tells you about all those cute accounts you can open for a grandchild's future educational needs.

Your decorator suggests that you redo your house so that everything will be childproof. You remind her that Baby will not live here but will simply enjoy occasional supervised visits (and you pray you are right).

Your coworkers conspire to offer you all their collective experience and advice on Lamaze, midwives, birthing rooms, breast-feeding, and going home from the hospital the same day. You sigh contentedly, realizing that you became a mother back in the good old days of doctors, five-day hospital stays, formula, and home nursing care.

The women in your car pool scream, "Oh my God, who would believe it!" and then add quickly, "Does that mean you won't drive on Tuesdays?"

And so it goes, as the news of new life spreads.

To some it is an economic windfall, because birth, like marriage, has its built-in costly rites of passage.

To others it is a criticism of their lifestyle.

But most people who hear about the upcoming event nod, congratulate you, and go back to their own made-for-TV life stories.

But not us about-to-be grandmothers. Because we have learned that the secret of life is new life. We know that in her own way, each one of us reinforces the values that came before, and at last we understand that this is why we are.

Baby Face

When Melody told her parents she was going to make them grandparents, they could scarcely contain themselves. Her father wanted to announce the news in lights on Times Square, and her mother wanted pictures immediately. But Melody and Tim managed to keep the parents in check until Melody was safely through the first trimester, and then the grandparents-to-be trumpeted their news to the Western world.

Of course the grandparents were on hand for the baby's arrival. They paced nervously at the hospital, and New Grandmother was at New Family's side the next day when they went home. New Grandfather ran countless errands for the parents. But New Grandmother, as she watched all the activity, was worried. It was obvious to her that while New Mother knew how to have a baby, she didn't know anything about caring for one.

How would she manage?

How would New Baby ever grow to adulthood?

New Mommy seemed to fall apart each time she heard the word "diaper," and phrases like "burp the baby" reduced college-educated New Mom to gibbering, jabbering responses.

"Do you think she knows what's going on?" New Grandfather whispered to New Grandmother as they huddled in the kitchen the third day.

"No," New Grandmother said. "She asked me again today how

to hold the baby. I keep assuring her that the baby isn't a piece of china—but really! Hold the baby! That's instinct, not tutoring."

It was not until the sixth day that New Grandmother called New Grandfather at the office. "Everything's fine," she crowed. "Our little mother is going to be just fine."

"How do you know?" New Grandfather asked apprehensively.

New Grandmother chortled. "Because she just walked into the nursery and told me I was doing everything wrong. The minute a daughter criticizes the old-fashioned way her mother does things, it means she's ready to do it herself."

New Grandparents Are on a Planet of Their Own (It's Called Heaven)

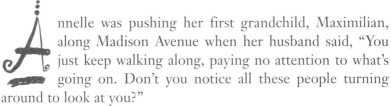

nnelle was pushing her first grandchild, Maximilian, along Madison Avenue when her husband said, "You just keep walking along, paying no attention to what's going on. Don't you notice all these people turning around to look at you?"

"Of course I see them turning to look," she answered smugly, "but they're not looking at me. They're looking at this beautiful grandchild."

"No, I don't think so," her husband answered. "You see, you are humming, and your humming is *so* loud—"

"What's wrong with that?" the new grandmother asked defiantly.

"Nothing, dear," her husband assured her, "but the tune you are humming is 'Hail to the Chief.' "

They are old friends and new grandfathers, so when they met on the street, they embraced and began telling stories about their new babies.

"You wouldn't believe—" one grandfather began.

"—what my grandchild looks like," the other concluded.

"Want to see a picture?" they asked in unison.

And so each reached into his wallet and took out a picture, and together they stood and oohed and aahed.

It wasn't until the grandfathers had said their goodbyes and were seven blocks away from one another that each realized he had never looked at the picture of his friend's grandchild. Each had taken out the photo of his *own* grandchild and admired it; the happy grandpas had never bothered to exchange pictures.

Grandfather was making a major presentation to an important client, so for luck he stopped by to give his new grandson a kiss and hug.

The family thought it was a very cute kind of grandpa thing to do, and even the baby seemed to like the visit so much that he reached out for Granddad to hold him.

Feeling happy, Grandpa went to the office and into the conference room. The client was there, and so were the charts and slides.

Grandfather stood to make his welcoming speech. He stretched his arms to encompass all the people in the room, and as he started to speak, everyone laughed.

He looked down.

A baby sock had fallen out of his sleeve.

Fashions of the Times

Just because she pushes a carriage, changes a diaper, and sits on command doesn't mean that a grandmother has to dress like someone out of the *Farmer's Almanac*.

But the unfortunate thing about fashion is that the people who can afford designer clothes (mostly grandmothers) find that they would have looked better in them thirty years earlier.

Short skirts when you're long in the tooth?

Frankly, when lengths began to go up and I saw my contemporaries rushing to buy short, I was amazed and wondered why the hurry.

"It's my last hurrah before the knees go," one grandmother

confessed. "You see, I've already lost the chins and the stomach."

Now don't get me wrong. I never questioned whether short short is adorable adorable. It is. It is. On skinny sixteen-year-olds, short short is cute cute.

But spare us the grandmothers who, instead of tummy tucks, are tucking their overdone bodies into underdone skirts. Little skirts on big girls simply don't cut it.

Of course, not all grandmothers are slaves to fashion.

Even grandmothers with good bodies often have good sense.

One day a grandmother I know was trying on a dress with more cleavage than dress. "Get it," the saleswoman urged. "It looks great on you."

The grandmother smiled and shook her head. "No. It's not what I had in mind for Grandparents' Visiting Day."

One grandmother concedes that her short skirts went the day her grandchild asked why she had so many blue lines on her legs. "That was when I realized," sighed the fashionable granny, "that I am too old to go short."

But most of us grandmothers figure we're not too old or too fat or too female to wear something that would truly shock our grandmothers. Trousers.

Whether they stay in or out of fashion, chances are we'll all stay in slacks, because for chasing a houseful of grandchildren, playing on the floor, or shopping for the eating habits of three generations, there's nothing like a grandma who wears the pants in the family.

Going Up in Smoke

She started smoking when she was sixteen, and no one was going to make her stop. So she lit up even when the whole world gave her fiery looks.

Despite loud protests, she smoked around her children, around her friends, on the golf course, and at parties. She smoked at the office and in elevators—even when the sign read No Smoking. She stopped flying when they banned smoking.

Then, at age seventy-eight, she became a grandmother.

"You can't smoke around our baby," the new parents said.

So Grandma, like a teenager, sneaked out back for a few puffs.

And then one day the parents said, "Sorry, but you have the smell of smoke about you. You can't handle the baby."

That was the day Grandma stopped smoking.

She wouldn't do it for her parents, her husband, her kids, or her coworkers. She wouldn't do it for friends, for convenience, or because it was the wise thing to do.

"What can I tell you?" Grandma muttered. "I'm nuts about the baby, and I said I'd do anything for a grandchild—so here's where I start."

Some smoking grandparents, however, need another kind of family nudge. . . .

Grandpa came to visit eleven-month-old Katie, gave her a kiss, and lit a cigarette.

Katie looked at him sternly for a few minutes and then clearly

said, "Moke!" and shook her finger, adding, "No, no, no, no."

Her parents had no idea where that originated—but you can guess where it ended.

Grandpa never "moked" anywhere near Katie again.

In Michigan, a four-year-old boy made such a fuss over smoking that he finally persuaded his grandmother to give up her thirty-year habit.

But it wasn't easy for Granny. Finally she went to the doctor for nicotine patches.

The next time her grandson came to visit, she told him proudly, "Grandma got some patches from the doctor, and they have helped her stop smoking."

The grandson listened thoughtfully, then said, "I wonder if he could give me patches so I'd stop biting my nails."

Grandma Coach

Grandmothers remember when prospective fathers were nervous guys who paced hospital corridors smoking cigarette after cigarette while their wives, off in some white-walled, antiseptic world, delivered their babies.

If you were a father in those days, it would have been easy to buy into the stork theory of childbirth.

How times have changed!

Now Dad coaches while his wife, the mother-to-be, cooperates, and *together* they have a baby.

When Karen learned she was pregnant, she and Darryl decided it would be "their" baby from the start. He'd coach her all the way—from the first contraction to the moment of birth. "We will bond with this baby in a special way," Karen promised.

Late one afternoon, Karen went into labor, and although Darryl ran to catch the next commuter train, Karen decided she needed immediate action. She called her mother to take her to the hospital and left word for Darryl to meet her there.

Granny-to-be not only drove Karen to the hospital but went along to the delivery room. When Darryl arrived, he rushed to the delivery room to coach his wife.

After a few minutes, Granny-to-be noticed that Darryl had turned pale green. "Darryl," she whispered as she tugged at his sleeve, "would you like to stand over here in the corner? I'll be happy to help."

And so Darryl went off to the sidelines, and Granny went into the front line. "Push," she commanded, and her dutiful daughter obeyed, just as she always had when her mother gave orders. Ten minutes later, Granny screamed, "It's a boy!"

The nervous father burst into tears. "I wanted a boy, but I was afraid to admit it," he cried.

It is now four years since that baby was born. Naturally, Daddy loves his boy with all his heart, but guess who really bonded with Brand-new Baby?

Grandma Coach, of course.

Frontline Grandma

When Cindy came to work at our office, she was engaged to be married but said nonetheless that she hoped this would be her job for life. I looked at her and smiled sweetly. Sure, sure. A young woman about to be married hopes this is her job for life? She never heard of having babies and 4:00 A.M. feedings?

Cindy did marry, and two years later she came to me and explained, "I want to be totally honest with you. We'd like to have a child, but I'll be able to continue working because even though my commute is two hours long each way"—four hours of travel a day—"my mother says that if I have a baby, she'll help. She lives close by."

I know Cindy's mother. She is a very lovely motherly woman, but at sixty-something, who can handle a newborn every day? We'll see, I thought. We'll see.

A couple of months later, Cindy came into my office and closed the door. Her eyes held a secret. "I'm pregnant," she said a little nervously, but proudly, "and I want you to know early so that we can make arrangements to keep the office running smoothly."

"What does your mother say?" I asked even before I wondered about the happiness of Cindy's husband, Marc.

"My mother says to count on her," Cindy replied.

Six weeks later, Cindy once more came into my office and

closed the door. She was obviously nervous. "I have good news and bad news. The good news is that I'm having twins. The bad news is I need a longer maternity leave."

"What does your mother say?" I asked again.

"My mother says that's swell. She loves babies."

We all love babies, I wanted to say. But every day? We'll see.

We didn't have long to wait.

Five months later, the boys were born, weeks ahead of their anticipated arrival.

Two boys, big and strong. Adam and Zachary.

"It's my family," Cindy crowed. "It's all the family I'll ever need. The complete family—A to Z."

"But what about Vera?" I asked. Vera is Cindy's mom.

"She's taking it very well," Cindy said.

It wasn't until the boys were past their first birthday that I had the nerve to call Vera. "How's it going?" I asked.

"I'm tickled to death," was her quick comeback. "I kind of volunteered for this job. I took care of my niece until she was three. I love all babies. These children are so special, and I just love them to death."

"But aren't they walking and getting into trouble now?" I asked.

"Oh, they're good boys. Grandpa Jim made a big gate in our family room just off the kitchen, and they play there."

"A gate? Have they been getting into things they shouldn't?"

"No, they're fabulous. Oh, sometimes Adam steals Zachary's bottle, but I make him give it back."

"But they're good boys?" I persisted.

"The best," she assured me. "They love magazines, and I show them the pictures and tell them that's Grandpop. They're such pretty little boys. I laugh all day with these babies."

"So you have no worries, Vera?"

"Just one. As you know, Cindy stays home on Friday. Well, there she is with the boys, so the first thing she does is get them up and dress them and take them out to a class. Then she brings them home and dresses them again and takes them marketing. Then they stay out for lunch, and next thing you know, they're over at the mall. With the kind of week she has and the work she does, I really worry about her on Friday, taking care of the twins. I think she overdoes it."

"*She* overdoes it!" I exploded. "Vera, that's one day. You have them all those other days."

"Yes, I do," she said happily. "Aren't I lucky?"

It's a couple of years now since I raised an eyebrow and dismissed in rather cavalier fashion the idea of Vera caring for one baby, much less two. I said wait and see. Well, I waited and now I see. I see how time and effort have made it possible for Vera to know and love these boys in ways most grandmothers never grasp; I can see how Vera's life has shifted toward a whole new exciting center.

And I can see why, even when she's most tired, Vera calls herself lucky.

Ten Ways to Make Your New Grandchild Love You

Forget whether the baby looks like you, your husband, or your uncle in Kalamazoo.

The only thing that really matters is how to make the baby love you, love you, love you.

Here are ten surefire ways to make sure a grandchild loves you, although it is possible you may alienate the child's parents for life:

1. Say "yes" no matter what the parents decree.

2. Throw away the clock when a grandchild comes to sleep over, and never insist on a curfew.

3. Teach your grandchild how to make chocolate milk shakes.

4. Promise the Eiffel Tower, a full set of the Encyclopaedia Britannica, and a laptop computer if Baby says your name before learning the names of the other grandparents.

5. Never discuss toilet training with the little darling or suggest that there is a thing called a bathroom.

6. Let your grandchild run wild at Toys "R" Us.

7. Permit the little darling to watch as much TV as he or she wants.

8. Never tell the dear child to smile at the camera because Grandpa is taking videos.

9. Do not tell the baby about your friend whose grandchild can do more tricks than the family dog.

10. Buy a lifetime supply of magnets and cover your refrigerator, inside and out, with the precious sweetie's artwork.

Part
Two:
∞∞∞∞∞∞

Miami,

Your-ami,

Her-ami;

or

my grandparents

the

tourist

attraction

The Short (Order) Life of Grandkids
on the Run

So they're coming to visit.

That's the good news.

The bad news is that you have to cook for them.

Well, maybe "cook" is too strong a word.

What you have to do is defrost and microwave for them. Or you have to happy box, juice box, or potato chip for them.

Because life is cooked to order for today's children.

When we grandparents were children, we ate what everyone in the family ate, or we went hungry.

The rules were not hard to follow.

When we had children, we bent the rules and, just for the children, served those universally recognized Kid Foods of their generation: hot dogs or hamburgers.

But for this newest generation, life is a Chinese menu, with one child ordering from column A, another from column B, and the third—who doesn't eat Chinese—from Dairy Queen.

Grandmother Ellen knew that each of her grandchildren had somewhat different ideas about eating. Still, she wasn't fully prepared for the variety show at mealtime when she went to visit her son and daughter-in-law for three days. Tootsie, the two-year-old, ate peanut butter but no bread. Tommy, her six-year-old brother, loved bread with jelly but no peanut butter. Andrew, the

nine-year-old, wouldn't eat any of the above. He lived instead on SpaghettiOs, bread sticks, and popcorn. "Don't you think you ought to get him to try some vegetables?" Ellen asked her daughter-in-law.

"You try," was the response.

Ellen decided to go home the second day instead.

Fran, on the other hand, has noticed that today's children often have sophisticated tastes. She has one grandchild who loves sushi, another who would live happily on tofu, and a third who refuses to eat any salad unless it's prepared with radicchio.

Anne, however, tells yet another food story for the contemporary family.

"My first grandchild is an adopted Korean boy. I noticed that he loved rice; all this child ate was rice. No potatoes. No pasta. I said nothing but assumed that this fondness for rice was genetic. I did think it rather amazing that a preference for food could be inherited, but like a good grandmother, I said nothing. Then, when my daughter had a birth child, who is Caucasian, I was

mystified. This child also ate only rice. And when yet another natural-born child came into the world and joined the family at the table, he, too, was a rice fanatic. Finally I figured it out. It was my daughter who was the rice enthusiast. My grandchildren ate rice because that's what my daughter cooked. My daughter never served potatoes. She didn't make pasta. All she made was rice. And I, with my three college degrees in anthropology and sensitivity to cultural differences, had assumed I had all the answers. That taught me that no grandmother has all the answers these days."

Then there is John, the five-year-old, who was going to dinner with his grandparents. "Grandma," he said, "let's not go to a slow-food restaurant."

"Wait a minute, John," said Grandma. "What's a slow-food restaurant?"

"Oh, you know," he told her. "The ones with menus—and you wait and wait and wait, and the food comes real slow."

Grandma got the picture.

They went to McDonald's.

Lunch with Grandma

a billion grams of FAT.

Joke by first-grader studying nutrition:

First-grader: What is the difference between a mother and a grandmother?

Mother: I don't know.

First-grader: A mother's dinner has three grams of fat, a grandmother's dinner has a billion.

A Is for Alex

StephanieAlexEmily is the way I think of the three children of my son, Rob, and his wife, Denise. Oh, I know the children, at nine, six, and two, have separate personalities; I do love them for their individual qualities: Stephanie is petite and athletic, and her perfect politeness seems as natural as her long hair; Alex likes to draw, is cuddly, and has the same kind of little matchstick body that his dad (now a sturdy man) once had; and Emily—well, Emily is undoubtedly the most perfect baby in the Midwest, mostly because whenever her parents say, "Kiss Grandma," she does.

Still, despite the obvious differences (and yes, I am guilty of that timeless granny practice of calling grandchildren by one another's names), I do think of them as a unit.

So when Rob decided to bring his son to spend a few days with me in advance of a family visit, I welcomed the chance to concentrate on Alex in a way I'm not able to do when my attention is divided among three children. I liked Rob's reason, too. "Alex needs a little bonding with his grandmother and time alone with me," he explained.

Eager to make the visit a success, I began my preparations almost before I'd hung up the phone. We'd go to museums. We'd shop. We'd go to restaurants. And then, so that Alex the Artist would feel special, I decided to write a little book, *A Is for Alex*, for him to illustrate.

I was so anxious to have Alex spend his time illustrating the book that almost the first thing I did upon their arrival was to read the book to Alex.

Rob loved it.

As for Alex, he liked it—sort of.

"See?" I explained as I flipped the pages. "There's your name on the cover, and you can illustrate it."

Alex pushed the pages away. "I don't want to illustrate it."

"Grandma doesn't mean you have to do it this minute," his father assured him.

Wrong, Rob. That's just what Grandma meant.

"You can do a page a day," Rob continued, not reading my mind at all.

Alex, on a quiet day, draws between ten and twenty-five pictures.

"But I don't want to do this, Daddy," Alex insisted. "Grandma," he asked, "do you have any plain paper?"

I went to my computer drawer and pulled out reams of plain paper.

"Thanks," he said. Then he took his paints and crayons, went to the kitchen table, and started to draw.

Hours later, I went to look at the pictures he'd created.

"What's this?" I asked, picking up one.

"It's a factory."

"How do you know about factories?"

"Our class went on a field trip to an apple orchard, and we saw apples picked; apples go into a machine like this."

"And this picture?"

"That's Belle and the Beast, Grandma. *Beauty and the Beast* is my favorite movie in the whole world. I saw it four times."

There were pictures of mountains ("We studied mountains"), pictures of Ariel and other mermaids ("That was a pretty good movie too"), castles he created, and rainbows he re-created.

By the time his siblings and the other cousins came to town, Alex had decorated the door of my fridge and a few walls with his artwork.

Me?

I'd learned the best lesson of all in getting to know grandchildren. Ask no questions, and you'll get all the answers you'll ever want. Instead of quizzing them, lead them to an activity, and through their involvement in what they do well, learn about their lives.

And even if you think they have a talent, don't program it.

I had assumed that since Alex likes to draw, he would want to be part of my book world, as an illustrator.

Wrong.

Alex is his own person who makes his own pictures, pushes his own pencils, and thinks his own thoughts.

One day I asked Alex where his ideas for his artwork originated.

"They come from a little pink place in my head," he announced quickly.

"Oh," I answered. I couldn't think of another thing to say.

"You have that same thing," he assured me. "Do you know what it's called?"

"Do you mean a brain?"

the
Billy, Jr.
retrospective
June - July

"Yes." He smiled. "Now, Grandma, all you have to do is use it."

So that's what I've been trying to do.

I have been trying to follow Alex's brainy advice, remembering not to try to program those who share my space and time. I'm trying to give room to those I love and allow them freedom to express themselves the way they want.

Who said being a grandmother was going to be easy?

A Little Old-Time Religion

Four-year-old Richard walked into the church and listened as his grandfather explained that this was God's house. Awed by the grandeur of the nave, Richard shook his head. "Wow!" he whispered. "God sure must be a very tall man."

Bobby was getting ready to go to church with his family. It was the Feast of St. Francis, the time of the blessing of the animals. "Grandma," Bobby began in a puzzled tone, "I'm worried about the animals. They're going to be so hungry."

"Why?" asked Granny.

"Because," he answered, "the elephants are so big that they'll probably eat all the communion, and there won't be anything for the little lambs."

"No, no, Bobby," Grandmother reassured him. "It doesn't work that way ... but," Grandmother murmured, "that is a thought worthy of St. Francis himself."

Samuel, age six, was sitting next to Grandmother at services in the temple. "The Lord our God, the Lord is one," the rabbi intoned.

"Grandma," whispered Samuel, "when will He be two?"

Two-year-old Jake was listening to his grandmother tell of the family plans for Christmas, when a thought struck him. "Grandma," he said, "wasn't Jesus lucky? He was born on a holiday, and he died on a holiday."

Mark was three years old when his pet lizard died, and since it was her grandson's first brush with death, Grandmother Marie suggested that he and an older boy in the family hold a "funeral" for the lizard. Granny explained what a funeral was—a ceremony where you said a prayer, sang a song, and buried your loved one. She provided the shoe box and the burial place in the backyard.

The boys thought it was a fine idea. And so they proceeded to the yard. The older boy said a prayer, then asked little Mark if he

wouldn't like to sing a song. With tears in his eyes, Mark clasped his hands, bowed his head, and belted out "Hit the Road, Jack."

She was squirming and wiggling throughout her cousin's baptism, and finally the little five-year-old girl turned to her grandmother and asked plaintively, "Do we have to stay for the whole show?"

That Granny Is Some Dude

P atti is one of those grandmothers with more children than house, and by the time the family had expanded, with one grandchild after another, the house had contracted.

It wasn't too difficult for Pat and John to accommodate their five children, so long as they came to visit one family unit at a time. But it was becoming almost impossible for the entire family to get together in one place at one time.

It was soon after the fifth grandchild was born that Patti realized that if she didn't soon create a Memorable Family Event, her California-to-New-York-by-way-of-Oregon grandchildren would never meet, much less bond.

So Patti went into consultation with her travel agent, and over the period of a year of looking, deciding, and negotiating, Grandmother Patti and Grandfather John decided that they would take the children and grandchildren for their first get-together to Dude Ranch, U.S.A.

By the time they arrived for their holiday, Patti felt confident. She had planned a week filled with events; she had tailored times for the babes in arms and booked riding and sports events for the older children. It would be a full, exciting week. We'll have memories, she promised herself.

The first morning Patti and John bounced into action early; by 6:00 A.M. John had finished jogging and Patti was dressed in her

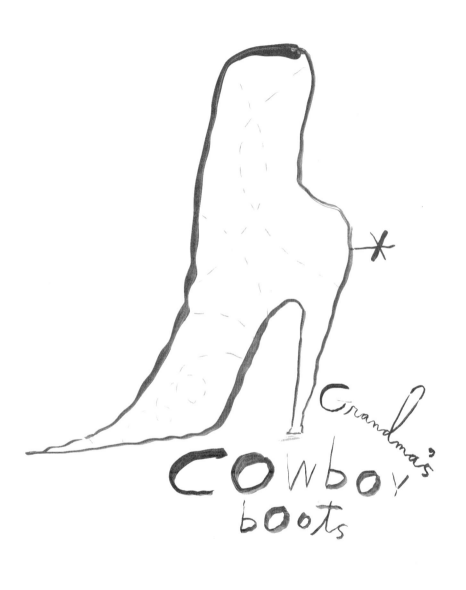

Grandma's COWboy boots

cowboy hat and jeans, ready for the Chuck Wagon breakfast.

By 7:00 A.M. this turn-of-the-20th-century granny dude was riding high in the saddle and looking pretty as a picture as the family reached the trail.

Grandma Patti smiled in satisfaction. At this moment she knew the work and worry had all been worth it. The children had survived that hard job of growing up. This long line of children and grandchildren.

Just look at the darlings!

The older grandchildren were riding docile, gentle horses, and the baby grandchildren—there were two of them—were strapped in backpacks on their daddies' backs.

When the family reached the chuck wagon site, they dismounted, laughed, and played as they breakfasted together and then headed back to the ranch.

They were within sight of the barn when son Joe's big cowboy hat flew off and sailed into the line of vision of his horse. The horse whinnied and broke into a gallop.

Joe, one of the daddies with a baby on his back, immediately clung—baby and all—to this formerly docile horse that was now running wildly in circles. "I'm holding on," Joe screamed to his wife as they sped by. Clutching the runaway, he remembered that when they'd taken the horse, earlier, he had been told that the saddle was loose, but the young assistant had said in that kind of casual Western style, "Not to worry. Your weight will keep that saddle in place."

Now, as the horse's speed increased, Joe could feel the saddle slipping. He tightened his grip and prayed a little, realizing that it was up to him to get his son and himself safely off that horse.

He braced himself for his move. He decided that at the next turn when the horse slowed slightly, he would use the slip of the saddle to slide off, roll, and—he hoped—protect his baby in the fall. Of course, Joe could communicate none of this to his weeping sisters and stoic wife as he flew by.

So when the family saw Joe and the baby fall, they were stunned into silence. In the distance they could see the horse running. Just ahead was Joe, rolling on the ground. But they could hear nothing. There was not a sound to break the desert silence.

Finally Joe stopped rolling.

And then there was a sound.

It was a baby's cry.

"They're alive," Patti screamed.

The breakfast ended with everyone in the emergency room of the hospital.

Joe hobbled in with his baby and heard the good news: No concussions. Nothing broken. Just minor bruises.

But the family was in terrible shape.

Frightened, confused, and shaken, the children wanted to go home on the next plane.

Patti looked at her watch.

It was eleven o'clock.

The next event, the White Water Rafting Lunch, was scheduled at noon.

What should she do?

Of course what she did was what every red-blooded, cool-headed grandmother hopes she can do when she's faced with decisions. She took charge.

"Pack up your water gear, kids, we're going rafting!" she announced. This granny did not traffic in fear, that contagion that spreads faster than a flu virus. Instead she bored through to her own steely center, and straight-backed and clear-eyed, she said to the children, "Change into your bathing suits. Uncle Joe's family will stay in their rooms, but the rest of us are going, and we'll have a wonderful time together."

She was right.

They did.

They went and had a fantastic time white-water rafting.

The kids screamed a little. But when they looked over at their grandmother, they could see that life was made of a bump, a jolt, an occasional splash, and some getting wet. Nothing to it.

Besides, they were Patti's grandkids, and each one knew that if she could handle all the tough stuff, so could they.

Anytime. Anywhere.

Did You See Your Grandchild Today?

The measure of love
Is not
How much
That child loves me
But rather
How much
I dare to love that child.

The Family Book of Quotations

Whether they're talking to grandparents or to friends (both real and imaginary) or just hanging out, there's no one more quotable than a grandchild.

Four-year-old Liza came to spend the day with Grandma, and toward afternoon she seemed a bit listless (greatest worry of any grandparent: the child will get sick while visiting), so Grandmother took Liza's temperature. As the thermometer was taken from her mouth, Liza looked up soulfully and asked, "Grandma, how do I feel?"

Conversations overheard by a car-pooling granny:
Girl I: I want a princess costume for Halloween, but my mother says I can't get it because it's too expensive.
Girl II: Oh, just ask my grandmother. She'll get you anything you want.

Boy I: Do you notice that everybody tells me I'm short? Don't they realize I already know it?
Boy II: I feel terrible.

Grandmother (anxious): Why?

Boy II: Stacy has a crush on me.

Grandmother: What's so terrible about that?

Boy II: Well, how would you like it if everyone told you Stacy had a crush on you?

Grandmother went to baby-sit her five-year-old granddaughter, and while the little girl was busy coloring, Grandma folded and sorted laundry. Puzzled, Grandmother turned to her granddaughter for help. "Whose navy-blue socks are these?" she asked. "I don't know where to put them."

"Oh," answered the little girl, blithely, "those go in the 'I don't know' pile."

Three-year-old Megan came to visit her grandparents, and she was immediately encouraged to sing a medley of her latest hits. She sang her little songs happily, and came to one of her favorites:

> "Mary had a little lamb,
> Its fleas were white as snow . . ."

Grandpa CEO

The nine grandchildren were all scheduled to go to lunch with Grandfather.

"Where'll I take them?" he asked one of the mothers.

"Burger King," she answered. "You won't be able to manage them no matter where you go, but if you're at Burger King, there are a million other screaming kids, so you won't feel so out of control."

Grandfather looked at her in amazement. Was this really how she thought the children would behave?

"Now, here's how to do it—" the mother began.

"Thank you, but I'll do it my way," Grandfather replied.

The big day came, and the ten of them—one grandfather and nine grandchildren aged three to nine—went to lunch. Afterward, when Grandfather had deposited the last of the grandchildren at home, Grandmother asked him how it had gone.

"Fine, just fine," he reported.

"Didn't Amelia want her bun toasted, and didn't Jeffrey ask for a burger with no meat, and didn't—"

"Stop," commanded Grandfather. "Here's how it was done. I got all the children together, sat them down, and gave them a menu I'd picked up in advance from the restaurant. Then I had each grandchild tell me what he or she wanted to order. I had my secretary do a seating chart—you know, the way we do for our board meetings—and I read the rules before we went."

"The rules?" Grandmother inquired.

"Rule one: No pushing. Rule two: No screaming. Rule three: No jumping up and down. Rule four: No changes once you order. Rule five: Use a napkin."

"This worked?" the surprised grandmother wondered.

"Of course it worked," the efficient grandfather told her. "I told them that this is how I run my business, and if it works in business, it ought to work in our family. And," Grandfather added proudly, "they all believed me."

"Maybe our children should try," Grandmother mused.

Grandfather shook his head. "They'd never make it work. The problem with parents is that they act like parents; you'll never get parents to believe that raising kids is really just another kind of business."

Relatively Speaking

You love the new little baby, and you unabashedly boast of the child's innate intelligence, budding beauty, and startling resemblance to your side of the family.

But if the truth be known, most of us grandparents don't really feel the full stirrings of that deep, forever love until a grandchild puts those little arms around us, plants a kiss on our cheek, calls us on the phone, or says "I love you."

Of course, the impulsive calls from grandchildren don't always mean they miss us desperately. Take the case of Grandma Anne

in Florida, who answered her telephone one day and heard a little voice trill, "Grandma, this is Ashley in California."

In answer to her wondering granny, Ashley explained that she had dialed Grandma by herself because her daddy was asleep and her mommy away. Grandma, delighted by the unexpected call, chatted on and on.

Finally Ashley asked, "Which grandma is this?"

"Grandma Anne," was the proud response.

With almost a sob, the little girl said, "Oh! I wanted to talk to my other grandma."

Phyllis played hide-and-seek with her grandfather, and—like many children—she covered her eyes in the belief that if she did, Grandfather couldn't see her. Grandfather, of course, played right along with her. Upstairs and downstairs he would look for Phyllis, under beds and in closets he would call her name. She loved their game. And so did Grandfather. But his favorite of all their hiding and seeking—the time he recounts to his friends—came on the day he went down to the basement to look for Phyllis, then chased back up the steps, to see her standing at the head of the stairway.

"Was I there?" she chirped.

Barry's grandfather likes his play times with his grandson, but

even when they go out to toss a ball, Granddad is not one of those cool, jeans-wearing guys. Instead he's more likely to appear in khaki pants and a dark-green sweater. A dash of color for Grandfather might be a maroon sweater. Still, Granddad was a bit nonplussed when his grandson turned to him and asked with the easy inquisitiveness of any four-year-old, "Granddad, why do you wear such boring clothes?"

"Boring," his grandfather sputtered. "Why are they boring?"

"Oh, I don't know," Barry answered. "Your clothes just don't speak to me."

Grandmother was teaching two-year-old Becky her colors: Which is red? What color is the sky? Becky was responding with the kind of alacrity that makes any grandmother seek a new definition of "genius."

"You are wonderful, Becky," Grandmother said, patting her beloved's curly head.

"No I'm not," Becky countered. "I am beautiful."

Grandpa picked up a multicolored ball and started asking two-year-old Kris the colors. Quickly and correctly, she identified them—red, yellow, blue, green—but when Grandpa came to purple, Kris was stumped.

"Well, what is it?" Grandpa prodded gently.

Kris thought for a moment and then piped, "That's something else."

Great-Grandparents: Our Timeless Treasures

There is humor, heroism, and a touch of forever in the lives of great-grandparents, for if grandparenting is the second chance at parenting, then think of the opportunities for great-grandparents to cross the generational time zones!

She loaded her supermarket basket in record time, then stood in line at the checkout counter. The young woman in front of her turned around, and her eyes widened as she saw twenty-two cupcakes, seventeen candy bars, and a children's video.

"Looks like your grandchildren are coming to visit," the woman commented.

"Grandchildren?" she sniffed. "My grandchildren wouldn't touch this stuff. This is all for my great-grandchildren. They're the ones for me to spoil now."

My mother is ninety-something and still parallel parks, goes to the mall, lives alone, has regular card games with "the girls," and plays the piano for her great-grandchildren.

"How are you doing?" I asked one day when I called.

"Just fine," she said. "You know, I talk to God every day, and the last thing I tell Him is, 'Thank you, but I'm not ready yet.'"

Her nine great-grandchildren aren't ready either.

His great-grandmother comes to visit often, and she likes to hold him on her lap. Looking at her one day, the little boy patted her lined face and asked, "Granny Joan, what did you look like when you were new?"

By the time they found Great-Grandmother's cancer, it was called incurable, and so her daughter came from her home in Rome and helped her mother make arrangements for the last months of her life.

They sold the house, found a hospice they thought suitable, and said the things a loving mother and daughter try to say to one another.

And then the daughter went back to Italy. But her thoughts were with her mother. Much as she wanted to talk to her, she dreaded telephoning. What was left to say?

It has been written that there is no truth comparable to sorrow.

So it was with an uncertain heart that the daughter called one day and, expecting the sounds of suffering, was surprised by her mother's lively, spirited tone.

Was it a miracle drug? What had happened?

"You sound so—so upbeat," the daughter exclaimed.

"I am feeling wonderful because I have a project," her mother reported.

"What kind of project?"

"Before I came here, a friend sent me a box of books, and one of them is a book for a grandmother to fill in. There are pages to write about my parents and childhood, about you and about all the children, grandchildren, and great-grandchildren in our family, and I cannot tell you what joy it gives me to relive the best—and sometimes the worst—of everything I have known."

"You sound so contented," her daughter said, as much to herself as to her mother.

"I am taking time to know where the sweet and the bitter are to be found, and I am putting it all on paper. This is a very exciting thing for me to do, because the very act of re-creating my life fills me with life. And because I am doing this, I know that I will not die. Every time you open this book, I will come alive. That's quite a wonderful thing for a great-grandmother to realize."

Naughty or Nice

The moment Grandmother heard his voice, she knew that her darling Felix had a problem.

"What is it, dear?" she asked quietly.

"It's almost Christmas."

"I noticed."

"I haven't been so good this year."

"You haven't?"

"No, I don't always do what Mummy asks."

There was silence.

"So, Grandmother, I want to ask a favor."

"Yes . . . ?"

"I know that Santa talks to adults, so I would appreciate it very much if you would call Santa and tell him that I really have tried to be a good boy and tell him that I must have those toys I asked him to give me."

Again there was silence, as Grandmother wondered how to answer, but before she could think of a response, her grandson added, "Oh, one more thing, Grandmother. In case Santa says no, would you please get me everything?"

This time Grandmother laughed aloud. She felt sure that her grandson would always get what he wanted, for already he understood a grandparent's role—to run interference for Santa.

Megan lives in Florida and goes to visit her grandparents up north every Christmas.

"What do you want for Christmas?" her grandmother asked by telephone one day.

"You can do anything I want, can't you, Grandma?"

"Absolutely," her grandmother assured her.

"Good," she said with some relief. "In that case, will you make sure it snows when I'm there?"

Richard went to the shopping mall with his grandfather to see Santa.

"Now, you go right up to Santa and tell him everything you want," Grandpop urged.

"No," said Richard.

"Come on," Grandpop coaxed. "Santa likes you. He'll listen carefully."

"I'm not telling him," Richard announced firmly.

"Why?" Grandpop asked.

"Look, Grandpop, Santa guessed right last year. He can do it again this year."

An Arizona grandmother sent her three-year-old granddaughter a Barbie doll for Christmas. So what did little Granddaughter

do first? Undressed the doll, of course.

Still, Mommy was surprised when her daughter, with tears in her eyes, came running, to show her doll. "Mommy," she cried as she pointed to Barbie's breasts, "something is wrong with her. She's growing elbows in front."

Adam was given a batting tee and kept trying to hit the ball—but nothing happened.

Finally Grandfather said the immortal words: "Adam, keep your eye on the ball."

So Adam dutifully got down on the floor and put his eye on the ball.

There's No Business Like Kid Business

Christopher wanted a dinosaur collection more than anything in the world, but his parents—after seeing that his dream gift cost more than $100—told the boy that it just wasn't in his future. If he wanted that kind of toy, he'd have to earn some of the money for it.

Christopher puzzled over the ways he might supplement his twenty-five-cent weekly allowance, but it wasn't until the family

visited Grandma and Grandpa in Florida that he came up with something. Chris's grandparents lived on a main route, where hundreds of cars whizzed by each day, so Chris decided to embark on what is often the first business venture of young boys and girls: he set up a lemonade stand and then, for good measure, persuaded Granny to bake cookies.

What hot, thirsty motorist can refuse a boy with a lemonade stand and home-baked cookies?

By vacation's end, Christopher had amassed a whopping $350. He went to the toy store and bought his dinosaurs, and when Grandmother asked what he planned to do with the rest of the money, he said he'd wait and decide.

It was some months later when, back at home, Chris's mother saw her son come out of his room wearing his best blazer and clean jeans. Mama knew that her dear little Christopher, even on the best of days, had to be bribed before he'd put on a tie, don a jacket, or wear jeans without a tear in them. And besides, this was a school vacation day. Mama was suspicious.

"What's up, Chris?" she asked with just a trace of motherly suspicion, for a boy who is unexpectedly good causes as much concern as the child who is deliberately bad.

"I'm going to lunch with my broker," Christopher replied.

"You are *what?*" his mother screeched.

Then Christopher explained that since he had $250 and knew that Mr. Brown next door was a broker, he'd called and asked him what to do with $250. Mr. Brown had suggested that Christopher come downtown and see what investing money was all about, and he promised to guide him.

Chris's mother took him downtown, delivered him to Mr. Brown, and mumbled, "It was just a little lemonade stand in front of his grandmother's house. What have we started?"

"Probably the next McDonald's," Mr. Brown told her.

Most children, however, get their first entrepreneurial experience selling Girl Scout cookies or bake-sale items for Sunday school or sports teams, so when an Illinois grandmother received a call from her granddaughter, asking her to buy some candy bars, Grandmother was curious about which cause and asked, "What are you selling them for, Katrina?"

There was a moment of silence, and Katrina answered, "Well, I can't give them away, Grandma."

Alexander the Greatest

Alexander, who lives in California, came with his parents to visit Grandfather and Grandmother in New York. One day he was in a taxi with his grandparents, and when the cab stopped for a traffic light, a ragtag woman approached and, with a toothless smile, put her hand out to the driver.

Grandmother just happened to have a dollar bill in her hand.

"Here," she called as she unrolled the window and handed the woman the bill.

The old woman nodded her appreciation.

Alexander, who observed this without speaking, turned then to the old, unkempt woman and blew her a kiss.

The cab drove on.

"That all happened in a twinkling," Grandmother reported, "but can you imagine the last time anyone blew a kiss to that woman?"

And now Grandmother wonders to herself and to Grandfather, "What can a family do to help a boy grow up without losing that sweet spontaneity?"

Huggin', Kissin', and All That Stuff

Tracy came to visit her grandmother, and in the first happy rush of reunion, Grandmother Joanne swept her granddaughter off her feet, covered her with kisses, and then echoed the fervent cry of every grandmother: "Do you have a kiss for Grandma?"

"Hold it, Grandma," the three-year-old cautioned. "If I'm overkissed, I explode. I'm small, and I can't hold that many kisses."

Erica was getting her grounding in manners from her mother. "You must say 'Please,' " Mommy urged as Erica pointed to the Barney doll she wanted. "And we say 'Thank you' when we get what we want. Those are the magic words," Mother continued. "We have a lot of magic words in life. Make sure you use them."

Erica nodded knowingly.

"Now," Mommy asked a few minutes later, "what is the first magic word we use to get what we want?"

Erica looked up, blinked her big blue eyes, and quickly said, "Grandma."

Grandmother Mimi came to visit, pinched the cheeks of her precious two-year-old grandson. "How was I lucky enough to get you for a grandson?" she asked coyly.

"I don't know," her grandson answered. "I guess you must have been first in line that day."

My granddaughter Molly was visiting with her parents one weekend, and the grownups, including Molly's big brother Max, were watching the World Series.

"I'm bored," Molly announced, and took herself upstairs to bed. Within a half hour she appeared at the door of the library, dragging her blanket. "I can't sleep."

I looked at my watch. "It's ten o'clock," I told her, "and if you

like, I'll go to bed now, and you can sleep with me."

"All right," Molly said in that "ye-e-e-s" voice.

The next morning, Max shook his head. "I can't believe it, Molly. You went to bed last night without your stuffed animal. It's the first time you ever slept without Kanga."

Molly looked at him, shaking her head. "Don't you understand, Max? I don't need an animal if I can sleep with a human."

Reach Out and Touch a Grandchild

From where I stand
To where you are
Are years of mystery
That we can never share—
Yet love and understanding
Can build a bridge
For us to cross
And so reach each other
In ways that matter
To us both.

In the old days, love and understanding were easier bridges to build because we all lived around the corner from one another.

Grandmother and Grandfather were down the block; aunts and uncles a town or two away. Now we are not only towns apart but continents away. We no longer can take the Sunday-afternoon ride in the family car to see Grandmother. Cousins grow up without playing with each other. So how do we bind ourselves forever to the grandchildren we so seldom see?

Chicken every Sunday or the weekly visit to Grandmother used to recharge the family batteries. Nowadays we have new choices—we can plug cellular power into the family tree.

The newest regular users of computers are turning out to be retirees who have their own code names and computer clubs and communicate directly via fax and modem with their grandkids, all of which makes today's grandchildren microchips off the old block.

A New York grandmother recently bought herself the ultimate grandmother present: three videophones, for her two children on the West Coast and for herself. On Thanksgiving Day, the family held two separate celebrations, one on each coast, and then spent part of their Thanksgiving together via videophone, displaying their turkeys, varieties of stuffing, and assortment of desserts. Those food notes, however, were not what made the use of the telephone most memorable. The real highlight of the family dinner came when seven-year-old granddaughter Ariel wished everyone a Happy Thanksgiving. In honor of the videophone, this California kid had used Kool-Aid to dye her hair blue.

The cousins definitely noticed her.

With the advent of the airlines' frequent-flier plans, some

families have their own flying clubs and accumulate mileage in a new-style family savings account. Members of the family draw on the account as necessary to bring everyone together.

Hotels now offer special packages not only for nuclear families but for "Grandparent Weeks."

While all this traveling is generally comprehensible to grandparents, our grandchildren are sometimes befuddled by unfamiliar terms—like the names of hotels. Mandy, age nine, was traveling in Canada with her family when they pulled up to a Four Seasons Hotel. "No," said Mandy emphatically, "I will not stay there. I know they'll give me winter, and I'm already too cold."

Other grandparents nourish relationships in novel ways.

A great-grandmother with a passel of grandchildren has a special day for one great-grandchild every week. A small gift is sent for that child, and helpful parents keep Great-Granny aware of the children's evolving hobbies, their favorite books and toys.

Another grandmother not only sends a gift to each birthday child but also writes a separate letter with an enclosed dollar to each of the other children in the house, so they won't feel left out.

A video-toting granny tapes herself having a conversation with the grandchildren, singing a song to them, or telling a story.

A cut-and-paste-type grandmother clips articles from newspapers and magazines about animals, music and adventures, and sends them with her comments.

One letter-writing grandmother corresponds with her grandchildren by asking specific questions and leaving room on the page for their answers. For good measure, she encloses a stamped, self-addressed envelope, because the only address children seem to have at the ready is "The North Pole."

But the grandmother who really makes her presence felt across the miles is the granny who reads children's books on audiotape, complete with directions ("Turn the page"; "Look at the funny tail on the dog"; "Who is in the tree?"). Then she sends the tapes and books to the child, so she can be the teller of bedtime stories to her long-distance grandchild.

With care like that, a child might be sixteen before he realized that Grandma wasn't right there at his side all those years.

Holding fast to history, strengthening the roots—that is the real job of grandparenting. We look for the time and space to bring our families closer. This is a scary world, but we know that if we seek each opportunity to make our love burn brighter, that love will light the path for the generations that follow us. Our daughters and sons now know that sweet, wistful love all parents know, a love born with the knowledge that life has its limits and only this moment is ours. Now our children are aware that they, too, must make the most of their time to be part of the timeless, unique family history that they are weaving.

So now our kids listen—no longer exhausted or bored by what we say—for they realize that in days ahead they may want to borrow a few pages from our survival guide.

We are aware that even though growing up is a painful process, grandparents can be a never-ending source of healing for punctured pride and fractured feelings.

We can be the spring of life, often without any awareness that we possess and pass on that energy.

We can serve as beacons even when we don't even know our lights are on.

And so we go, making families work in the era of two-career families, no-job households, and failed marriages, and despite illness, handicaps, and heartache. We are grandparents, and our true talent is the ability to overcome all disability.

Sex, Style, and Grandchildren

I just phoned to see how all of you are, but you sound terrible. Anything wrong with the children?"

"They are all healthy and in school. They're happy as can be. Mom, it's me. I'm the one who's upset."

"What's the problem?"

"Victoria. The problem is Victoria, my darling twelve-year-old who thinks she's twenty-seven."

"What happened?"

"She wants to know why she can't go to boy-girl parties when parents aren't at home. She keeps complaining, 'You don't trust me.' "

"Oh, that. You did the same thing at her age."

"Mom, I was thirteen."

"And that's your only problem?"

"No. Yesterday Victoria told me she's going to shave her head and put a stud in her nose."

"I remember when you dyed your hair orange and had your ears pierced."

"Mom, I was fourteen."

"Oh, of course."

"Now Victoria wants to use my car. I have to keep telling her it's against the law."

"That's what we used to tell you, and you drove around the drive anyway."

"But I was fifteen—practically sixteen."

"Oh."

"And listen to this part: Victoria goes with just one boy. I don't know why kids today can't have parties with parental supervision and boys and girls just getting together without thinking they have to pair off."

Grandmother said nothing.

"So, Mom, what do you think?"

"I have only one thing to say: Welcome to the club."

A Stranger in Our Midst

It was evening, and the day-long cold rain counterpointed the glow of the living room fireplace. We were in the country with our family, and while the weather hadn't measured up to expectations, the rest of the weekend had.

In the library, five grandchildren—fed but wide awake—were watching a movie, and in the kitchen the two sets of parents and I were talking and laughing as we prepared the grownups' dinner. One couple was marinating chicken, another fixing pasta, and as I took out serving plates, I felt at peace, for I had that mother's sense of contentment that comes when you know where your children are—and you approve.

Suddenly Max appeared in the kitchen. "There's a man at the window with a flashlight," he said, his big eyes wide.

"Are you sure?" his mother asked. Six-year-olds in the midst of play sometimes confuse reality with imagination.

Marisa, aged ten, followed him into the kitchen. "Oh, there's a man," she confirmed. "We all saw him, and he's looking in the window at us."

We stood frozen for a split second, and then all of us, children and adults, raced to the living room. Outside in the heavy downpour stood a man with an umbrella. He looked fortyish and was slightly balding—all in all, a rather ordinary-appearing fellow.

"Don't open the door," advised one father grimly. So I

motioned the man to the window next to the front door. "What do you want?"

"My car just blew a tire on the road over there," he said.

"Ask him what road," urged the other father.

"I guess it's Route 174," he said.

I turned to the family gathered behind me. "There is no Route 174 over there," I told them, trying to sound brave.

"I have my young son with me," the man said, "and we'd like to come into your house to make a phone call." He shoved the child, a boy about ten, into my view.

I moved to open the door.

"No," shouted the four younger adults in unison. "Never open a door to someone you don't know."

"Tell him you'll make a call for him," one mother said.

"Ask him where his car is and tell him that you'll call the police for him," instructed her husband.

So that's what we did.

We let the man with the umbrella and the little boy try to find their way back to their car—or to another house—and we walked slowly into the kitchen.

"I'd have let him in," I said. "That's such a wicked rain."

"But this isn't the first house he'd have seen if his tire blew out on the main road," said one of the young men. "Why did he pick this little deserted street? Why leave the main road?"

"We just couldn't let you open the door," explained one of the mothers. "We have five young children here, and we want them all to understand that they must never let a stranger into the

house. They just had a very good lesson. They saw that you can help without risking your family's safety."

All this took place far from the everyday violence that's so seamlessly woven into our expectations of urban life. But ever since this event, I've told the story to different groups and asked what they would do. Without exception, people old enough to be grandparents would open their doors and make the stranger welcome, while those who are still parenting insist that they would never open a door to admit any unknowns.

Sometimes I wonder what happened to the man and his son.

Did the police find them in the car?

Was there truly a car with a blown tire?

Did another family on our street believe the story and let them in?

What bothers me most is what this story says about life in a world where one's first instincts for helpfulness are tempered by fears for safety.

For if we cannot offer concerned care at our door, then we, parents and grandparents together, must all go out of our way to prove it exists.

Why Do You Love Your Grandparents?

Grandmother Gail went to Grandparents' Visiting Day, and each child was asked to stand and tell: "Why do you love your grandparents?"

The reasons were predictable: "They take me to lunch" . . . "They let me play the piano very loud" . . . "They buy me presents" . . . "They are good to me" . . . "They let me stay up late" . . . and on and on.

Finally it was little Leah's turn. She stood and faced her class. "I love my grandmother because she takes me to work with her. She owns two nice stores, and she is the president. I am very proud of her. I am going to be chairman of the board when I grow up, and then we will have a whole lot more stores."

Look out, world. Here comes Leah.

Part three:

FAMILY TIES;

oR

unSnarling the married,
unMarried, almost
married woRLD
of
Parents,
children
and grandchildren

Where's Grandpa?

I stood at the door as they came up the steps, his grand-children and mine, in a kind of happy lockstep. They call themselves The Cousins, and so they are. Their relationship is made not by nature but rather by us, by Lee and me. Our marriage made them cousins and made us a family.

And as I watch, my eyes fill with tears. I know that their feelings for one another are there for life.

It is years now since Lee died, enough years so that baby Sarah, born only weeks before his death and held only once by him, is now a kindergartner.

Lee has not been here to see the good things that have happened to our children. He did not see his son Zev move into a secure life of his own, nor did he live to see his daughter Carol fulfill her long-ago promise to him to go back to college and get her degree.

He did not live to see my daughter Kathy write her first book, or to talk politics and swap Philadelphia stories with her husband, Henry.

He never saw Denise and Rob's third child.

Yet although Lee is not here, his presence is always with us. We toast him. We speak of him.

And we speak of him in the present. We cook his recipes, and we tell his stories, and we remember his friends. When life was

ours, we used to cook Thanksgiving dinner together. It was a big event because it always brought the family together. Once, Lee turned to me and said, "You have to promise me that no matter what happens to me, you will always have our Thanksgiving, and you will keep all our family together."

I keep my promise each year.

But even though he doesn't know it, I keep the promise each day too.

We all do.

Because we know that love and loyalty aren't like family silver. We can't unwrap and polish our emotions one day a year.

So we do it a day at a time.

And we think that's just the way Lee wants it.

The Good Old Days

Most grandchildren take one look at us and decide we must have been born at some point between Cro-Magnon man and the Civil War. They tend to think of us the same way as the young grandson who asked his granny at dinner one night if she had gone to school with Abraham Lincoln.

"No," Grandmother answered a bit peevishly. "Why would you think so?"

"Because you knew so many dead people," he responded.

Sometimes grandchildren find difficulty bridging the time span between the generations. And so, from time to time, do grandparents.

Matthew was visiting his grandma, and she was telling him about life when she was a little girl. "The iceman used to come around on a truck, and my mother would put a card in the window telling how many pounds of ice we needed that day. But the best part," Granny explained, "was when the iceman would stop in front of our house and start chipping away. All of us kids would run out to catch the chips and let them melt in our mouths."

Matthew listened attentively. "Were you poor, Grandma?"

"Not really," she replied.

"Oh, I understand." He nodded. "Money wasn't invented yet."

A nine-year-old visiting granddaughter asked if Grandmother wouldn't play a new game on the computer with her.

"I'm so sorry," Grandmother apologized, "but I don't know how to use a computer."

"Oh, Grandma," sighed the nine-year-old, "didn't you go to second grade?"

The three-year-old came into the den, where Grandmother was looking at a picture of herself holding the halter of her horse. It was a photograph taken when Granny was exactly the present age of the little girl's mother.

"Grandma," asked the little girl, "whose horse is Mommy holding?"

"That's not your mommy," Grandma explained slowly. "That's me. Gramma."

There was a pause, and finally the little voice piped, "When did you turn into that other girl?"

Them's Fightin' Words

Remember what it was like when your children lived at home? When life was an endless series of sibling shouting matches punctuated by the dreaded words "You do that once more, and I'll tell *her!*"?

Who was *her?*

Wicked old mom, of course.

But something rather delicious happens to many of our children once they grow up and move out. Somehow they seem to find that their siblings have improved with age.

Polly's daughter called just a few weeks ago to say that she and

her husband had decided not to sleep at Mom and Dad's house when they came to visit. Instead they planned to drive fifty miles to sleep on a sofa with bad springs at sister Bonnie's.

"I wanted so much to have the children with me," confessed Polly, "but the sisters wanted to be with one another, and that is a far greater reward for a parent than having a child choose you. I never had a brother or a sister, and I always thought it would be wonderful to grow up and find a big sister in my life. Then as I got older, I looked around and realized that not all brothers and sisters love one another. I decided to try to keep our girls close-knit, and so we planned a lot of family events—holidays, vacations, special treats. Always we emphasized the sisters. And I guess it has worked; but boy, were there times when you could have fooled me.

"When I think how they used to fight over everything—drying dishes, skirts, money, privileges . . .

"So when a daughter says she'd rather drive fifty miles for an uncomfortable bed than come home to Mom, I know I have no complaints. But when they were little—whew!"

Maybe this perspective is what makes it possible for us grandparents to shrug when we see our grandchildren argue about toys and treats, raise their voices and stamp their feet in exasperation at their sisters' and brothers' behavior.

We can even laugh about seven-year-old Freddie, who, when he gets especially annoyed with his sister and wants her to stay out of his room, leaves a note on her door saying,

"Dear Felice, I hate you. Love, Freddie."

Because we know that this, too, shall pass. Over the years doors will open and angry notes will give way to embraces.

In the end, the echoes of childhood past will herald the grace notes of the future, and many of these children—like the feudin' and fussin' generations of siblings who preceded them—will bond for life.

Or at least that's what we dream.

Tradition

Tradition is simply habit with a fancy name.

Still, tradition is the flour in the roux, the cement in the pillar, the okra in the gumbo.

And in this busy world of the two-working-parent family, it has never been more necessary or more important to maintain traditions. And who gets the job of initiating and maintaining tradition? You guessed it! Grandma, that's who.

The holidays come complete with built-in tradition. If Christmas and Thanksgiving had not been created, however, some grandparent somewhere would have thought them up. But beyond the calendar holidays there are those special days that grandparents create.

An innovative grandmother in Scottsdale has decided to take each of her grandchildren to Washington, D.C., once they reach the age of twelve. Why is twelve the magic age? "Because," Grandmother responds, "at twelve they are old enough to remember, and after twelve I don't want to deal with their hormones."

Two widowed grandmothers in Detroit, each with a four-year-old grandson, agreed that since they couldn't offer the boys male bonding, it might be fun to plan grandmother-grandson days from time to time. So these inventive grandmothers planned active day trips to places appropriate for the boys, everything from children's theater, movies, and museums to the zoo and swimming lessons. All four conferred in advance and made the plans; as one of the grandmothers said, "We became the authors of our own adventures." As the boys grew older, the grandmothers took them overnight to historical places that would intrigue eight- and ten-year-olds. And now that the boys are in their teens, the grannies are planning to give their grandsons their first taste of Europe. They'll spend a winter poring over catalogs and creating an itinerary together. "It's a unique tradition," one of the grandmothers admits, "but once you're a widow, you have to face the fact that life isn't the Waltons, so you'd better make up your own stories."

In Philadelphia, a grandmother and grandfather have once-a-month Saturday-night sleepovers with their three preschool grandsons. And on Sunday morning, the boys climb into bed with their grandparents, to play Sandwich.

Explained Grandmother, "The boys can be roast beef or cheese or turkey—anything they want—and then they tell us what to add to the sandwich. If they say mustard, they get Grandpa to tickle them; if it's ketchup, it's Grandma. Best of all is coleslaw, because that's two tickles. These kids think it's the greatest thing in the world to play Sandwich with us. But of course, we knew they'd love it. It was their father's favorite game too."

In our family there is the tradition of weekends to celebrate the August birthdays of four granddaughters two years apart in age. With sleeping bags, cots, and a bed for the smallest child, we've gathered annually at our house in the country. Now that the children are older, they sleep in the barn and put up signs to tell the grownups to stay out. It seems that at an early age, children learn that exclusion is the first sign of inclusion.

Golden Wedding Time

*T*he same four couples have been playing bridge for fifty years, and this past year they celebrated the golden wedding anniversary of one couple with an all-day-and-evening round robin of tennis and bridge.

Their bridge is much as it was, no better and no worse. But what about the tennis? a friend asked. Seventy-somethings playing set after set of tennis?

"Oh, we did fine," Grandfather Paul recounted. "But don't think we play only with each other. Tennis is a sport for all ages. Why, just a few weeks ago I played singles with my teenage granddaughter, and I whipped her three sets straight. As we walked off the court, she shook her head in disbelief. 'I don't understand it, Grandpa,' she said. 'I've beaten better players than you.'"

Katie, whose parents are both twice-married, listened as Grandpa told her that he and Grandma would soon be married for fifty years.

She shook her head in wonderment. "Gosh, Grandpa. You mean you never had another wife?"

Grandpa was leaving the house, and he gave a goodbye kiss to Grandma and their four-year-old grandson, John, who was visiting.

After Grandpa left, John turned to his grandmother. "I'd like to ask you something," he said earnestly.

"Yes?"

"I just saw Grandpa kiss you, and I wondered . . . are you guys married yet?"

The GAR
(Granddaughter Approval Rating)

Annemarie went to visit her grandmother, and to her surprise, Grandma's boyfriend, Leonard, wasn't there, as he usually was. But Annemarie asked no questions. She went straight into the living room to play Nintendo.

Pretty soon Grandma came into the room with a man Annemarie had never seen. "This is my friend Gregory," she said to her granddaughter. Annemarie looked up, grunted "Hi," and went back to her Nintendo.

An hour later, Annemarie waved goodbye to Grandma and Gregory. When Annemarie got home, Grandma phoned. "Why," she asked, "were you so abrupt with my friend Gregory? I've told him so much about you, he really wanted to meet you."

"Look, Grandma," said the eight-year-old. "I like Leonard. I'll always like Leonard, so don't introduce me to any of your new friends."

A few weeks later, Grandma recounted the story to another dating granny. "I tell you it's enough to make me go back to Leonard," she sighed.

Samantha, age eight, was reading her copy of *Seventeen* magazine. "Mom," she asked, "tell me about dating. What's it like?"

Her mother looked at her and shrugged. "Don't ask me. I can't remember. Ask your grandmothers; they're the ones who still date."

Grandma had a lunch date with eight-year-old Jill and noticed that the child was unusually quiet. Finally, looking over the top of the maraschino cherry on her chocolate sundae, Jill asked, "Have you heard the news, Grandma?"

"What news, dear?"

"About Grandpa. He's going to live with that woman he's been seeing."

"Oh, yes," Grandma answered easily. "I heard the news, but you have to remember that Grandpa and I have been divorced for a number of years now, and we always wish each other well. She's a very nice lady, and I am sure she will make him happy."

"But, Grandma, they're going to live together. What do you think about that?"

"I think that if they love each other it's just fine," said the thoroughly modern granny.

Her granddaughter put down her spoon. "You do? Well, I want you to know that I am shocked."

"Shocked? Why, dear? Don't you believe that when two people love each other—"

Jill put her elbows on the table and looked into her grandmother's eyes. "Don't you get it, Grandma? Grandpa is setting a very bad example for us grandchildren."

He's No Grandpa, He's My . . . He's . . .

Welcome to the wonderful world of Grandma's dear male friend.

And hello to Grandpa's lovely female friend.

These friends present a conundrum for parents everywhere. What should the children call a grandparent's longtime companion?

In Michigan, a grandmother's dear friend, Paul, was given the name Grand Paul by her grandchildren.

A woman in Oregon suggested that a gentleman friend be consulted before he is given a name. (Her suggestion was Fo-Pa, unless the man in question considered that a faux pas.)

My friend Eva is called Vava, which has turned out to be just fine with everyone, and it came about because a little boy couldn't pronounce Eva.

Once married, people find the problem simplified.

A Florida woman's father married a woman named Dora, who was promptly called Grand Dora, a name bestowed by one of the grandchildren.

In yet another family, a grandchild was urged to call Grandpa's friend "Fairy Godmother," since she acted as a second godmother. And guess what! Not long after that she became "Grandma," which is one proof of where good deeds can lead.

The Steps of Grandparenting

I t wasn't a first marriage for Migs or Bill, so they came together not only with old dreams but with older children, children who were half past childhood and well into their own lives.

Migs had pleasant—even cordial—relations with Bill's son, but she always thought of him first as "Bill's son." Then one night Bill's son called to invite his father and stepmother to dinner with him and his wife.

105

That night the young couple told Bill he was about to become a grandfather, and Migs would be a grandmother.

Migs nibbled her salad and rolled the word "grandmother" around in her head but not her heart.

And then the mother-to-be brought out a sonogram and showed the outline of the unborn child to the older couple. "That was the minute I knew I was hooked," Migs confessed. "It was also the moment when I realized that this young girl had lost her own mother and was turning to me to play a real role."

When Benjamin was born, Migs and Bill took the next plane to see the child.

"We've been running ever since," Migs admitted. "I am hopelessly, wildly, madly in love with Benjamin, as is his grandfather. I buy him cards from all over the world, and with each card I send bubble gum, stickers, or chocolate—the three things I know I can use as bribes. Oh, I'm shameless. I do whatever I can to get his attention, to secure his love. We had a party for his first birthday, invited all the family—including my parents, who had to get on a tiny plane during a violent electrical storm, but they wouldn't miss the celebration. And it isn't that we're romanticizing this child; a romantic is someone who loses sight of the real world. We are in total touch with reality. Benjamin is a special child; we love him with all our hearts, and we want him to know that. My own grandmother was a memorable force in my life, and I hope to have that kind of role in the life of this family. By the way, my definition of a contemporary grandmother is any woman on an airplane with more shopping bags than luggage. I think grandmothers are the original bag ladies.

"I suppose I should tell you one more thing. Since Benjamin's birth, my own son and his wife have had a child, and we are mad for this smart and talented little girl too. We love our new granddaughter dearly—but Benjamin is our first grandchild, and you know how we grandparents are with firsts.

"How do we both feel about being step-grandparents? Don't be silly. There are no steps with grandparents. Didn't anyone ever tell you we are the ones who invented unconditional love?"

Not Quite a Grandmother

When she chose her vocation, she opted for the religious life—but when the time came to take her vows, Patricia McCarthy realized that she was not ready to enter the convent; the world was too much with her.

And so she returned to her home in New York. By then, however, "home" had scattered. Patti's brother was in New Orleans, her parents were gone from the city. Still, New York had the strongest sense of a place called home, so that was where she settled. She culled lists of old friends, made new ones, and the years rolled by.

Jobs changed; men came and went; and even though she eventually found her place in the work world, Patti didn't meet any man she wanted to marry.

Did that mean she was never to know the joy of mothering? Not necessarily.

Both her religious upbringing and her family had taught Patti that love can be given regardless of marital status. Over the years, she came to forge a special bond with the daughter of her brother. Wendy was a precious child who, from the time she was old enough to be put on a plane in New Orleans, came to New York for what she came to call "Aunt Patti times."

Patti recalls those days with a laugh in her voice. "Can you imagine that I climbed to the top of the Statue of Liberty? Me, who's afraid to get up on a ladder! Of course, I loved doing anything I could for Wendy. She never asked for things and was always so appreciative of everything. I'll never forget the time her grandfather gave her money for her visit to New York and she insisted on taking me to dinner. I thought she ought to spend the money on herself, but she was so persistent that I let her take me to the little neighborhood restaurant that we considered 'ours.' She was so proud to pay the check herself."

Wendy grew to young womanhood, made her own way, and, like most of us, faced both good and bad times, for no matter how much we love our children, there are heartbreaks we cannot intercept. Wendy's first marriage ended tragically with the sudden death of her young husband. Then Wendy married again, only to have her soldier husband sent to the Persian Gulf just as hostilities began. That Thanksgiving, feeling confused and sad, Wendy did what she had done so often as a child. She got on a plane and went to New York for an "Aunt Patti time."

Not long after the young soldier's safe return, the couple called

Aunt Patti with the news of Wendy's pregnancy.

Wendy's baby came two weeks early and, unlike most new babies, arrived not at 2:00 A.M. but at 2:00 P.M. Patti was surprised by the news as she sat at her desk, but she was even more surprised when immediately after assuring her that the new baby and new mommy were fine, the new daddy put Wendy on the phone.

"Aunt Patti," she said in a strong, sure voice, "we'd like to ask a favor of you."

"Anything," her excited aunt promised.

"Will you let us name the baby after you? May we call her Patricia McCarthy Beron?"

For a moment, Patti could not speak. When words finally came, all she could do was sputter, "What? Why? Are you sure? You—you really want to do that?"

Yes, yes, and yes, they told her. Yes, they were sure. Yes, this is what they wanted. Yes, they hoped she would agree.

Patti told these dear children how honored she was. Then she put down the phone, and the tears came streaming down her face. "I left the office and cried in the elevator. I walked home and kept on crying. Then when I got home I cried some more.

"Oh, I know I'm not her grandmother," Patti said quickly. "I won't confuse the roles, but you just wait until that little girl needs someone to walk up the steps of the Statue of Liberty, and even though I still can't bear going above the second floor, you'll see me running up those steps, and you'll know for certain that an aunt can be a grandmother."

The Grandparent-Go-Round

I t's a mad whirl, this world of the grandparent, because just when you expected life to go into neutral, you're suddenly on a thirty-six-speed bicycle—going uphill.

Some of us end longtime marriages.

Some of us face unexpected widowhood.

Some of us remarry and create the new all-American amalgamated family.

Our family situations are a result of birth, of change, of choice, and of chance—but forget all that.

The thing to remember is that every grandparent, regardless of how he or she came to this stage, shares certain basic truths. This is only a small sample of some of the truths of which grandparents of every shade and stripe are aware:

No man under the age of sixty is anxious to be a grandfather, but every woman over the age of fifty counts the days until she is a grandmother.

Just about the time your children look down on you, along comes a grandchild to look up to you.

Grandparenting is a wonderful time of life. Finally we can have the ice cream without first eating the vegetables.

Grandparents are like everyone else; they just have more pictures.

A grandparent's work is done when the grandchildren are all good friends.

Grandparenting is a second chance to shape the future in our image.

ANSWER: No matter what the child does, one complains and the other brags.

QUESTION: What is the difference between a parent and a grandparent?

Part Four:

Heart-Strings

The Birthday Card

nce, my grandmother sent me a birthday card, and I kept it for years. I took it out whenever I felt dumb, ugly, and sad. (Is there a girl who has lived long enough to become a woman who didn't go through times like that?)

And on the days when I felt my worst, I would know that even though my teachers and the other kids didn't appreciate me, somebody did.

I don't know when I lost track of the card, but I never lost the verse it contained; I still play it in my head when I can't see beyond the rain on the window.

> Birthdays come and birthdays go,
> The years fly by, 'tis true,
> But to me the dearest, sweetest day
> Was the birthday that brought you.

The Grandma Dress

When I was a little girl, I thought there was only one grandmother dress, and all grandmothers wore it. They just took turns.

The dress was worn for everything from weddings to funerals. It was black, and made of stiff material, and it featured a high neck around which a grandmother hung her gold locket or pinned her cameo. The waist seemed to wander on this dress; sometimes it moved near the armpits, sometimes it roamed to the hips, and sometimes there was no waist at all. The sleeves, however, were ever-present, long and often buttoned.

It was known as "the good black dress." So far as any of us knew, there was no such thing as "the bad black dress."

Well, our grandmothers in their black dress should see us now. Today's grandmothers probably own at least one black dress, but the similarity ends right there. Today Grandmother's black dress just may have a neckline that plunges to where Grandma's waist used to be. And our lengths? We go to wild lengths, we grannies of the nineties. We can be long enough to trail the ground. We can be so long that we look as if we're characters in a Russian novel. And we can be just a wisp of fabric, not a hem but ahem!

Just the other day, I wandered into a fashionable store, and there was a whole floor of black dresses. I looked around and thought that if it weren't for the prices (did my grandmother ever

118

pay more than twenty dollars for a dress?), Grandma might feel right at home in this sea of black.

And Grandma would definitely feel at home when she saw this generation of grandchildren, because grandmothers of all ages know that while the fashions on our backs may change with the years, the fashions in our hearts remain unchanged.

Whether we wear it buttoned to the chin or zipped up the back, the little black dress will never cover up a grandmother's love.

How Grandparents Learn to Love

There is a picture of my son
That sits upon my desk.
In it he is seven.
And I am—
Well, I am his mother.

It is only a snapshot,
Not one of those studio glamour shots,
But I prize this photo above all others
Because the day is young and green,
And so are we.

I am seated on a garden chair,
And my little boy is cradled on my lap,
Recovering from
Too much or too little
Childhood.

I weep each time I look
At us
Enfolded in this pose forever,
While all about,
Life continues to unfold.

Somehow that sweet little picture
Touches me like music,
Just as music often photographs
Times too precious to forget.

So when the still air fills
With strong sounds of the past,
I am not surprised
To feel the strum of old chords
As the heart skips back
In time.

My son, held silently
For all these years,
Has shown me that,
With eyes closed,
I can hold fast to
The children that my children were
And so see and feel the way
To enrich, enfold, and celebrate
Another generation of our love.

The Water View

My friend John used to visit his grandmother at the family home on Long Island Sound, and he well remembers watching Grandmother walking on the beach and then contemplating the view from a chair.

But time and that thing we call progress soon took their toll. After a while, three huge smokestacks were built on the opposite shore, and John was sad to have his grandmother's view spoiled. One day when he was visiting, he took a walk on the beach with Grandmother.

"It's too bad they built those three smokestacks to spoil your view," John said, certain he was articulating the disappointment she had not expressed.

"Smokestacks?" She harumphed. "Smokestacks indeed. There are no smokestacks. We now have three beautiful lighthouses."

John admits that since that day he has looked for the lighthouses and avoided the smokestacks.

Look Who's an Expert!

When I was a little girl and people asked what I wanted to be when I grew up, I never answered, "A teller of grandparent stories," because back in those days I thought people were born grandparents. I assumed that I was born a little girl; my parents were born my parents; and my grandmothers were born *my* grandmothers—so how could I ever get a call from a child of mine who would say, "Mom, you're going to be a grandmother!"

But life does happen to all of us. What surprised me was that life happened to me so soon. When I was told I was going to be a grandmother, I was thrilled, but in my heart of hearts I didn't feel old enough to be a grandmother. I still wore my hair long and my skirts short (more or less, relatively speaking). I still worked and danced and played tennis (more or less, relatively speaking). Besides, I knew that to many people, "grandmother" meant old, used, and spent. I realized sadly that that was what it meant to me too. No matter that some of my best friends were already grandmothers; I just didn't look forward to grandmotherhood the way I had looked forward to mothering. I was sure that "grandmother" meant the end. Little did I know that it encompassed beginnings—the beginnings of dividends on the investments of a lifetime.

But the very night my first granddaughter, Stephanie, was born, I learned the true meaning of "grandmother." I wrote a

column in *Good Housekeeping* about Stephanie's birth, and this is part of what I wrote:

> *I went immediately to the maternity floor waiting room, where all our family was assembled, and I heard those wonderful words: "It's a healthy girl, born ten minutes ago."*
>
> *Moments later, in her father's arms, the baby came to meet us.*
>
> *To my shock and amazement, I burst into tears. But not just ordinary, run-of-the-mill tears. This was old-fashioned, heartrending sobbing. For in that moment I was touched by every new life that had preceded this new one.*
>
> *My father, dead before even my son was born, was there. So, too, were my grandparents, great-grand-parents, uncles, aunts, cousins. In a great, convulsive tide I was swept back to my beginnings—child, young wife, mother.*
>
> *I was filled with the enormity of that sense of belonging, all of us, each to the others. We are bound by our own inexorable, non-ending saga. We are the human story. We are us. And now she is us. And only God knows what lies ahead of us—and all life.*
>
> *No wonder I cried inconsolably.*

Well, the response to that column was so overwhelming that I realized I had struck a nerve—a grandmother nerve. I had unlocked a secret women had been longing to tell one another. The secret was that we were all kind of shocked that it was already our turn to be grandmothers. But now that we were, we wanted to say those things that assure us that life is meant to be lived, that each birth has a reason of its own. One reader wrote to say that her mother had sent her the column the day her child was born. Another woman had the column read at her mother's funeral. Unknowingly I had written a celebration of both the beginning and the end of life.

The response gave me the confidence and impetus to move forward and devote even more time and effort to updating the dowdy, dull images of grandmothers.

And so began my chronicling of grandparenthood.

What I've learned through my writing is that as grandparents, we have not lesser but greater roles to play in the family drama. Now it is up to us to instill the faith, maintain the traditions, keep the engines oiled and the spirits high.

The rewards are almost without measure, especially when something happens to make us realize that we grandparents do make a difference.

Lee was so smart about our family; he wanted our Thanksgiving tradition to continue whether he was there or not, and so it has.

Indeed, this last Thanksgiving was an epiphany of sorts for our family.

A few days after our old-fashioned family dinner, I received a note from Heidi, my darling stepdaughter-in-law (now, there's a nineties relationship for you), and she wrote in part:

"Thank you for the wonderful, warm, and loving Thanksgiving this year. It was really picture perfect—I will never forget sitting by the fire in the cozy living room with all of us together in such perfect contentment. Times like that can only happen through years of standing together in the face of whatever life brings—then suddenly there is this precious moment when everything stops and we can savor the peace of such seasoned and simmered unconditional love and support. *Our* lives just wouldn't be the same without it."

As I read Heidi's letter, my eyes filled; I knew then why we grandparents must remain the keepers of the promise.

And maybe the best way to do that is to try to live and love the moment, limit the criticism, and when the skies get dark, bring on the sunshine just by saying, "You wouldn't believe what my grandchild did. . . ."